VELOCIRAPTOR VS. BULL SHARK

Gareth Stevens
PUBLISHING

BY CAITIE MCANENEY

Please visit our website, www.garethstevens.com. For a free color catalog of all our high-quality books, call toll free 1-800-542-2595 or fax 1-877-542-2596.

Library of Congress Cataloging-in-Publication Data

Names: McAneney, Caitie, author.
Title: Velociraptor vs. bull shark / Caitie McAneney.
Description: New York : Gareth Stevens Publishing, [2019] | Series: Bizarre
    beast battles | Includes index.
Identifiers: LCCN 2018005941| ISBN 9781538219430 (library bound) | ISBN
    9781538219454 (paperback) | ISBN 9781538219461 (6 pack)
Subjects: LCSH: Velociraptor–Juvenile literature. | Bull shark–Juvenile
    literature. | Animal behavior–Juvenile literature. | Animal
    weapons–Juvenile literature.
Classification: LCC QE862.S3 M3338 2019 | DDC 567.912–dc23
LC record available at https://lccn.loc.gov/2018005941

First Edition

Published in 2019 by
Gareth Stevens Publishing
111 East 14th Street, Suite 349
New York, NY 10003

Copyright © 2019 Gareth Stevens Publishing

Designer: Katelyn E. Reynolds
Editor: Monika Davies

Photo credits: Cover, p. 1 (bull shark) Premium UIG/Universal Images Group/Getty Images; cover, p. 1 (*Velociraptor*) Antracit/Shutterstock.com; cover, pp. 1–24 (background texture) Apostrophe/Shutterstock.com; pp. 4–21 (bull shark icon) mtmmarek/Shutterstock.com; pp. 4–21 (*Velociraptor* icon) rikkyall/Shutterstock.com; p. 5 Stocktrek Images/Getty Images; p. 7 Franco Banfi/WaterFrame/Getty Images; p. 8 Christian Masnaghetti/Stocktrek Images/Getty Images; p. 9 Michael Moxter/Picture Press/Getty Images; p. 10 Daniel Eskridge/Stocktrek Images/Getty Images; p. 11 Narchuk/ Shutterstock.com; p. 12 JOSE ANTONIO PEAS/Science Photo Library/Getty Images; p. 13 AquariusPhotography/ Shutterstock.com; p. 14 W. Scott McGill/Shutterstock.com; p. 15 Matthew R McClure/Shutterstock.com; p. 16 Esteban De Armas/Shutterstock.com; p. 17 Ciurzynski/Shutterstock.com; p. 18 lucag_g/Shutterstock.com; pp. 19, 21 (bull shark) Jose Angel Astor Rocha/Shutterstock.com; p. 21 (*Velociraptor*) Michael Rosskothen/Shutterstock.com.

CPSIA compliance information: Batch #CS18GS: For further information contact Gareth Stevens, New York, New York at 1-800-542-2595.

CONTENTS

Words in the glossary appear in **bold** type the first time they are used in the text.

DEADLY DINOSAURS

Velociraptor is a predator **legend**, even though these dinosaurs have been **extinct** for over 70 million years. *Velociraptor* had a long, bony tail and a mouth full of sharp teeth. It also had claws at the end of its short arms and a curved, sharp **talon** on each foot.

Velociraptor had a lot in common with birds, as they also had feathers and hollow bones. *Velociraptor* was small compared to many other dinosaurs. However, don't mistake this dinosaur's smaller size for weakness. *Velociraptor* was a fearsome predator!

VELOCIRAPTOR WAS KNOWN FOR ITS SPEED. IN FACT, THIS DINOSAUR'S NAME MEANS "SPEEDY THIEF"!

BEASTLY BULL SHARKS

Bull sharks are some of the most dangerous sharks on Earth. They're found in both saltwater and fresh water. They're also very aggressive, or ready to attack.

Bull sharks get their name from their squared **snout** and bullish personality. These sharks often hit their prey with their snout before attacking.

Bull sharks are known for eating nearly anything they can find. That includes smaller ocean animals—and even other sharks. You don't want to mess with a bull shark!

 BULL SHARKS OFTEN SWIM IN WARM WATERS AND CAN BE SPOTTED NEAR COASTS.

A LOOK AT SIZE

In movies, *Velociraptor* looks bigger than it actually was. Its body was only about the size of a turkey! These small dinosaurs likely weighed up to 33 pounds (15 kg).

 LENGTH OF *VELOCIRAPTOR*:
UP TO 6.8 FEET (2.1 m)

LENGTH OF BULL SHARK:
7 TO 11.5 FEET (2.1 TO 3.5 m)

Full-grown
bull sharks
can weigh
200 to 500 pounds
(90.7 to 226.8 kg).
Female sharks are larger
than male sharks.
　Bull sharks are bigger than
Velociraptor. They win the size battle!

TOP SPEEDS

Velociraptor ran on two legs. Some **paleontologists** think it could have run at a speed of 24 miles (38.6 km) per hour. Its top speed may have been even faster, though it would've only run that quickly for short distances.

TOP SPEED OF *VELOCIRAPTOR*: 40 MILES (64.4 KM) PER HOUR

Bull sharks use their strong tail to swim. Their pointed pectoral fins help them turn quickly through the water. Even so, they aren't the fastest sharks. Their average speed is only about 5 miles (8 km) per hour. But, they can double their speed in short bursts!

11

STRENGTH IN NUMBERS

Velociraptor may have hunted in packs. Paleontologists have found piles of *Velociraptor* bones that show more than one of these dinosaurs dying while hunting. This likely means *Velociraptor* hunted with a team, which would have given it a serious **advantage** in a fight.

 VELOCIRAPTOR'S HARD TAIL LIKELY KEPT THE DINOSAUR BALANCED AS IT HUNTED PREY.

BULL SHARKS OFTEN HUNT IN MURKY, OR VERY DARK, WATERS. THESE SHARKS HAVE GREAT HEARING AND A STRONG SENSE OF SMELL, WHICH HELP THEM FIND THEIR PREY.

Bull sharks are usually solitary hunters. That means they prefer to hunt alone. But sometimes, two bull sharks may hunt together to trick prey.

WHICH WEAPONS WIN?

Velociraptor was armed with many **weapons** for a fight. It had a huge, curved talon on each foot that hooked its prey. The dinosaur's sharp claws and **serrated** teeth ripped prey apart.

VELOCIRAPTOR'S WEAPON COUNT:

- AROUND 30 JAGGED TEETH
- THREE CLAWS ON EACH HAND
- SHARP TALON ON EACH FOOT

Bull sharks have a huge mouth full of sharp teeth. Like many sharks, they have several rows of teeth. Shark teeth are triangle-shaped and jagged. Bull sharks have the most powerful bite of all sharks!

FOOD CHAIN FIGHT

Next, let's look at each animal's prey. This gives us a sense of the size of animal they could take down. *Velociraptor* was a carnivore, or meat-eater. It often ate smaller animals, tearing apart prey with its sharp teeth.

VELOCIRAPTOR'S DIET PROBABLY INCLUDED:

" SMALL ANIMALS, INCLUDING REPTILES, AMPHIBIANS, AND MAMMALS
" INSECTS
" SMALL, SLOW PLANT-EATING DINOSAURS

A BULL SHARK'S DIET CAN INCLUDE:

- DOLPHINS
- SEA TURTLES
- SQUIDS
- CRABS
- OTHER BULL SHARKS
- ANYTHING IT CAN FIND!

Bull sharks are also carnivores and will eat anything they can hunt down. However, these sharks usually eat bony fish and stingrays. In a contest for biggest prey catch, the bull shark wins!

17

THE SURVIVAL TEST

Which animal is the greatest survivor? Like all dinosaurs, *Velociraptor* died out millions of years ago. Paleontologists have a few ideas why dinosaurs might have gone extinct. However, dinosaur extinction is still largely a mystery.

 SOME PALEONTOLOGISTS THINK THE EXTINCTION OF DINOSAURS WAS RELATED TO **CLIMATE CHANGE** OR ILLNESS.

Sharks are some of the few survivors from dinosaur times. Shark **ancestors** lived more than 400 million years ago! Survivors must adapt, or change, to fit new conditions. Bull sharks are very adaptable, and they win the survival test.

19

ONLY ONE WINNER

It's time for the beast battle! Which predator do you think would win?

Velociraptor had sharp talons, claws, and super speed. However, the bull shark is a much bigger—and hungrier—predator. This shark's teeth-filled **jaws** could snap *Velociraptor* in half!

We will never know for sure who would win in this beast battle. *Velociraptor* was a land animal, while the bull shark lives in the water. However, the bull shark is alive today—and that's the ultimate victory!

THESE ANIMALS HAVE NEVER REALLY MET! WHO'S YOUR CHOICE TO WIN THIS IMAGINARY BEAST BATTLE?

GLOSSARY

advantage: something that benefits a person or thing

ancestor: an animal that lived before others in its family tree

climate change: long-term change in Earth's climate, caused partly by human activities such as burning oil and natural gas

extinct: no longer living. Extinction is when a whole species is no longer living.

jaws: the bones that hold the teeth and make up the mouth

legend: someone or something known for doing something very well

paleontologist: a scientist who studies the past using fossils

serrated: having sawlike points along an edge

snout: an animal's nose and mouth

talon: one of an animal's sharp claws

weapon: something used to fight an enemy

FOR MORE INFORMATION

BOOKS

Hopper, Whitney. *In Search of Bull Sharks.* New York, NY: PowerKids Press, 2016.

Pallotta, Jerry. *Who Would Win?: Hammerhead vs. Bull Shark.* New York, NY: Scholastic Inc., 2016.

Riehecky, Janet. *Velociraptor.* Mankato, MN: Capstone Press, 2015.

WEBSITES

The Bull Shark: No Shrinking Violet
sharkopedia.discovery.com/types-of-sharks/bull-shark/
Learn more about the aggressive bull shark and then test your knowledge.

Velociraptor
kids.nationalgeographic.com/animals/velociraptor/#velociraptor-hunting-nest.jpg
Get to know *Velociraptor* with National Geographic.

INDEX